A TRAVELER'S HAIKU

Original poems in English

by

JAMES W. HACKETT

The Hokuseido Press
Tokyo

A TRAVELER'S HAIKU

http://www.hacketthaiku.com

Other books by the same poet:

HAIKU POETRY, VOLS 1-2 (1964/6) HOKUSEIDO PRESS
(TOKYO)

HAIKU POETRY, VOLS 1-4 (1966/8) JAPAN PUBLICATIONS,
INC. (TOKYO)

THE WAY OF HAIKU (1968), JAPAN PUBLICATIONS

BUG HAIKU (1968), JAPAN PUBLICATIONS

THE ZEN HAIKU AND OTHER ZEN POEMS OF J. W. HACKETT
(1983), JAPAN PUBLICATIONS

30 ZEN-HAIKU (1994). ENGLISH, WITH GAELIC VERSIONS BY
POET GABRIEL ROSENSTOCK, ILLUSTR. PUBL: AN CUMANN UM
HAIKU, DUBLIN.

LE CRI DU FAUCON (1996). FRENCH TRANSLATION BY
PATRICK BLANCHE, CALLIGRAPHY BY YURIKO SEKO. PUBL:
VOIX D'ENCRE, MONTELIMAR, FRANCE

Published by The Hokuseido Press, Tokyo
http://www.hokuseido.com
ISBN 4–590–01164–6
First Printing, 2004

Printed in Japan

This book is dedicated to my beloved golden wife Patricia, devoted lifelong companion who gallantly shared the Way, and made my poetry possible.

JWH

Many thanks Rich
for being such a
good friend —

Jim Hartlett

CONTENTS

AUTHOR'S NOTE

At its best, travel helps us transcend the insularity and hubris which can distort and limit our understanding of the world. While inspired by global diversity, this collection of haiku (and its related genre, senryu) is offered in recognition of the universal spirit we all share.

So as you join in these travels, vicariously co-creating those haiku that are most vivid for you, keep in mind that:

"All of us are haiku poets in so far as we live in the present moment."

R. H. Blyth, haiku scholar (1898-1964)

ACKNOWLEDGMENT

To Mrs. Koko Kato, whose dedication to haiku and haiku poets worldwide is gratefully acknowledged by the author of 'A Traveler's Haiku'

A TRAVELER'S HAIKU

PACIFIC NORTHWEST
Glacial sunrise . . .
within a web full of dew
bouncing about

Pool's too deep to stand,
but it's worth treading water
for the summit view

Building a campfire . . .
suddenly sent straight to hell
by front page news

From life in this world
spider runs over ashes
right into the fire

Long night of storm . . .
Now on a trail reflecting dawn
and the goal beyond

The peak looms above,
but roots and rocks in the trail
hold the eye

Switch-back trails be damned,
this mossy log commands
　　the summit, and more

Vanish as they will
each fallen needle lends
　　its form to the snow

On a glacial trek:
warming every defile
　　— the wake of dragons?

Hail drums the tent,
but the summit now flavors
every sip of tea

(Squire Creek)
Tangled up in roots
and dancing with the current,
an old hook and line . . .

From enso* shadows
wheeling over the streambed
a whirlpool unseen

*A ZEN CIRCLE

4

Worth the climb, this view
beyond the ramshackle dream
of Father's gold mine . . .

NEW ENGLAND
Morning Mozart . . .
and gradually through the mist
an autumnal world

Seems that some bird
has run amuck in the snow
under this old pine

Dark forest pool:
searching in and around —
a last shaft of sun

NEW MEXICO
    Derelict farmhouse . . .
Creaking round with blades shy —
    the haunting of it

FLORIDA
    Hurricane's eye . . .
Ev'ry blade and bloom
    genuflecting stillness

Doing a ballet
upon the sidewalk scale:
   a friend of flavor

Takes one, for others
on the walk to stop and watch
   two flies tango

(on viewing TV)
   'Victory at Sea'. . .
Mid bobbing heads: that book
   in the teeth of one?

Tampa swallows
upstage the sunset that sends them
on maneuvers

Humbled to silence . . .
This Tampa Bay moon rise
itself a haiku?

MEXICO
Patriarchal palms
pelicans, and stinging ants:
Acapulco Zen!

(Acapulco)
Hurricane years, yet
still they stand, lending grace
to the ocean sunset . . .

(Cancun)
Tony beach hotel . . .
Searching between washes of surf
local 'snowbirds'

Cabo San Lucas . . .
Moths on siesta decorate
the cool toilet wall

(Yucatan Jazz Cruise)
Seniors jitterbug*...
Their wild prototypes join in
on the glass windscreen

*1940S DANCE

On a bobbing buoy,
trying to scan the depths
with an open gullet

❖   ❖   ❖

(San Francisco)
  The 'paragon' species?
Driving hell-bent down tollways
    in an S.R.O. world

  Master's sudden laugh!
Sign beside the freeway:
    'Self Storage Here'

(Airport runway)
  All may not be lost . . .
A line of ducklings just stopped
    the taxiing jet

(in flight)
    From her little dog
all groomed, ribboned, and perfumed:
    cat-box breath

    Scene from six miles up
midwest fields full of circles —
    Ben Nicholson's* career?

*PAINTER OF GEOMETRIC FORMS

❖   ❖   ❖

Beijing rush hour . . .
horse and cart heading home,
driver fast asleep

Dancing dragons . . .
One soars off through Beijing smog
to the Western Hills

A stone-grown thistle
halfway up the Great Wall,
resting butterflies

Great Wall Sheraton . . .
changing lobby bulbs atop
a tall bamboo rig

(to a hotel clerk)
'How ancient your dream,
to leave the Capitol for the wilds
of Sichuan'

Beijing tea mart . . .
A coquettish smile brings him
boxes of ginseng

Tiananmen wind . . .
the way gusts whip all the flags
into a roar of red

(Tiananmen rally)
Waiting for tots
in a chalked grid: Mickey Mouse
and all his friends

Temple of Heaven . . .
Foreigners seem from outer space
to provincial eyes
(1990)

Priest's 'halo' denied,
his guest's deformed *namaste**
is taken — and crushed . . .

*NAMASTE: A GREETING OF
PRESSED PALMS
MEANING 'I HONOR
THE DIVINE IN YOU'

Glee, then loud applause
from the monastery garden —
a snake, chased to freedom!

(*Shanghai*)
　High rise construction . . .
cut and roped into riggings,
　the Pandas' forest

Ancient Tao garden . . .
Looming faintly through the smog
　new China's high rise

Climbing a 'moon' bridge
to share the blossoming dream
　of an old mountain soul

White garden walls?
A Chinese riddle, resolved
    by the rising moon

Pavilion empty,
the old Shanghai gardener
    dances with herself . . .

(West Lake dawn)
    Out of nothingness
Sesshu*-like forms slowly emerge
    unto peaks of the Sung
* JAPANESE ZEN PAINTER —1600S

(Hangzhou)
  West Lake pavilion:
on the wall, carefully framed,
  a rare slab of stone

  Climbing 'Buddha Mount'
a millipede on the trail
  gets a lift from my wife

  Chan temple entrance . . .
Screened within a great vessel,
  blooming lotus

Hangzhou tea garden . . .
pure Tao, this tufa* rock
sculpted by the sea
*POROUS ROCK

(Suzhou)
Temple of Han Shan:
from just pointing skyward,
poet and priest rapport

Lined up to revere:
five hundred golden arhats,*
no one, anywhere . . .
*A BUDDHIST SAINT

20

Templed — with tourists
taped chant, and idoled in gold:
mountain master Han Shan!

Imperial canal . . .
Now with ev'ry boat, a wake
of black, littered muck!

Deep China rail:
my reading Tang poetry aloud
warms staring eyes

Bell tower strangers:
priest and poet beyond words,
laugh and embrace!

A stream of ponchos
cycling past stalls of trinkets
and sweet desperation

(Sichuan hills)
Wild-eyed and laughing
he points to his ecstasy
while pleasuring himself

(Guilin)
Famed river tour:
viewing landscapes of the Sung
— with loud, swilling locals

Flooded rice paddies:
way out, stranded on a dike
barking unheard . . .

❖   ❖   ❖

FRANCE
Mid Paris grandeur:
flowering sills and rooftops
'la   France profonde'*

*THE COUNTRY SPIRIT

On Pandemonium's gate:
*'The Louvre is Satan's palace
on free Mondays'*

(Normandy)
Cherbourg chateau* —
Watching moated swans
erase Nazi reflections . . .

* GERMAN OFFICERS' BILLET

At Omaha Beach . . .
from old bunkers of Nazi gall
    the stench of piss

(At Nohant*)
    It's not your guises
but your 'cosmic eye' that holds me
    M. Chameleon

*ESTATE OF G. SAND & F. CHOPIN

Provence market day —
a child with one kitten left
    her misty smile . . .

For full use
of your comic genius —
'*Salut, M. Parrot!*'

Arles amphitheater . . .
sharing Caesar's marble niche
rooted valerian blooms

Caesar's Triumphal Arch
spotlighted now, and wreathed —
by belching trucks

BRITAIN
    Wincing for Windsors
but admirably Franciscan
     his garden tête-à-têtes . . .

IRELAND
    In a drizzling world
the bonnie brogue, wit, and song
     of Erin's welcome!

    At day's end
busy as the pub it graces,
    sweet honeysuckle

ITALY
    Ancient amphitheater*. . .
splitting aura, ears, and stone
    a teen's boom box

*GREEK THEATER ON SICILY

(Rome)
    A living nightmare:
graffiti on the Colosseum
    'El Duce Lives!'

SPAIN (Granada)
    Moorish aires — fugal
with flowers, fountains, and birds
    Alhambra gardens

(Kyoto)
    Shrill heat . . .
beetle runs over waves of sand
    to the temple's shadow

    Just a 'photo-op'
to teens — perching atop the rocks
    at Ryoan-ji*
              *FAMED SAND GARDEN

    Mid manicured shrubs
and designed gravel, my spirit's
    longing for the wild

Daitoku-ji monk:
'Garden's full of symbols'
   — rocks and sand protest!

(Daruma Dera)
   In Ten Bull* Garden:
the priest echoes infinity
   with each 'Ah, so desuka!'

* DARUMA—IS THE JAPANESE NAME FOR BODHIDHARMA
   (THE FIRST ZEN PATRIARCH). THE TEN BULLS ARE
   SEQUENTIAL STEPS IN THE REALIZATION OF ONE'S TRUE
   NATURE. EACH STEP IS REPRESENTED BY PLANTINGS IN
   THE TEMPLE'S GARDEN.

30

The reclining Buddha?
Now — finally realized —
life's a divine dream . . .

A living sutra*
uniting birds, beasts, and man:
golden fields of rice . . .

*BUDDHIST TEACHING

Amidst devotees
before a large gold Buddha —
my welling sadness

(Miyajima)
On a temple path
doubled over by decades . . .
the hidden price of rice?

Standing on loose trash:
wobbling in my view finder
a torii-framed* sun!

*SHINTO GATEWAY NEAR THE SEA

Heavenly bamboo
ever growing through the gloom
its old canes create

32

(Kamakura)
   Look: fly after fly
pirouettes to my curry, then leaves
   with a loud buzzzzzz

Completed by Heaven . . .
Daibutsu's* serene face
   streaked with compassion
          *GIANT OUTDOOR BUDDHA

Over Blyth's* grave:
an offering of mourning rain
   muddy knees, and brow
         *THIS POET'S MENTOR

(Ryutaku-Ji*)
A live 'pagoda'
with a heavenward will —
timber bamboo

Garden, my sutra*. . .
cicada moments deepen
zendo stillness

Solemn ceremony —
til the head-to-head meeting
of priest and gaijin!*

(Ryutaku-Ji)
   Resting my koan*. . .
the zendo's visiting roshi
   a lone cicada . . .

*WORD OR PHRASE USED
IN ZEN MEDITATION

Heavy summer night . . .
even the lone cicada sputters
   into silence

(At a flute master's home with Soen Roshi)
   'But Roshi, the crab
eats everything in the sea —
   and we eat* the crab!'

*AND WE ALL DID!

A wordless sutra
wafted by butterfly wings —
blooming gardenias

Clinging to a twig
now full of nothing but light —
the end of summer

Come! The mountains
have hazed into a painting
and tea is served . . .

'*Dew no longer gems*'
the old Roshi once told me.
True now — and yet . . .

This ancient teapot —
the way it leaves an enso*
upon everything

*ENSO (A CIRCLE OF ENLIGHTENMENT)
SIGNIFYING "SUPREME" IN ZEN
PAINTING

❖   ❖   ❖

(British Columbia, Pylades Island)
Aerie ! And beyond
a fugal dawn . . . at one with birds
the sea, and itself

Fear not, mollusk,
the 'Jaws of Life' couldn't
part you from your rock!

(Valdes Island)
Nest of eaglets . . .
perching wrens join the flies
to take in the show

Now from the sea, beach,
and even the eagle's eye —
   a blinding glare

(Pylades Island)
   'Hush! Defect from the war
— and foxy Zen, too — but believe
   this full rising moon!'
         (1968)

Shouting farewell
to my red-robed friend ashore:
   'Buddha's a shit stick'

Long torrential night . . .
Hued drops poised on every twig
    filigree the dawn

Noisy woodpecker's
penance: to look heavenward
    with every swallow

(Alberta)
    Banff to Jasper peaks:
beyond even Bach — but one
    with the soul of raga

Granite-clear, deepened
by eons of summit flow, —
the chill of kensho!*

*SEEING INTO ONE'S
TRUE NATURE

Waterfall pool . . .
Watching a last shaft of sun
collect rainbows

❖   ❖   ❖

GREECE

Parthenon grandeur
floodlit high above a TV
masted 'Mark Tobey'*

*AMERICAN ABSTRACT PAINTER

Acropolis cats!
Competing for attention —
the Parthenon

Athens bus tour . . .
Not even for a microsecond,
Schliemann's* home

*EXCAVATOR OF TROY

Now — all but drowned out
by the throngs at Delphi:
   its oracular birds

(Delphi Museum)
   To my whispered
'This silver bull has gold balls'
   some gal adds *'You're darn right!'*

(Mycenae)
   Enter 'Lion's Gate,'
then it's worth the climb — this view
   Agamemnon* knew
            *KING OF MYCENAE

(Gulf of Corinth)
    Islet hut
a stone's throw from shore:
    the soul that so abides?

    Let's also give Faust*
his due: from Corinth's bauxite mounds
    to this stratospheric view
        *HUMANKIND

(Greek Isles)
    Embering our wine,
the Aegean, and sky into one —
    Santorini sunset

TURKISH COAST
How eloquent amidst
grasses, poppies, and turtles . . .
'the glory that was Greece'

Gilding the thrill
here where Alexander* wintered:
wild-flowered ruins
*KING OF MACEDON

AUSTRIA
Wheeling together
over a withered cornfield —
the squawks between

(Innsbruck)
    Alpine gravestones . . .
'Killed at Stalingrad 1942'
    — while touring, or what?

GERMANY
    Pandemonium hell!
Satan lives here in Munich
    during Oktoberfest

    Munich tour bus:
the guide always whispers
    down streets of the rich

Passed in silence — the hall
where Hitler and Chamberlain
signed 'Peace in our time'

Oktoberfest melee!
On empty streets nearby,
shibui* autumn . . .

*SUBTLE AESTHETIC (JAPAN)

SWITZERLAND
Picnic in the sky . . .
wildflowers, wine, cheese, and
airplanes fly below

Travel cautionary:
'Quibblers avoid Switzerland,
Uzi owners, all'

HUNGARY
Bored on the Danube:
Look! One orchard tree's got
the 'Heebie Jeebies'*

*THE JITTERS

ROMANIA
Warm caressing waves
of Black Sea moon . . . even here
a boom box echoes

Bucharest airport:
from lobby palm to window,
again and again

❖   ❖   ❖

INDIA

Somehow flowing
every which way, like the Tao,
Delhi's 'traffic yoga'

The rajah hobnobs,
pausing frequently to quaff
from his silver flask

Khajuraho airport:
two wild monkeys preview
the erotic art to come

A morning raga:
rice planting — reflecting
saris and the dawn

Our Jaipur bedspread:
woven into the brocade
weaver's glaring stare

(Kerala)
   Jogging to work
clutching huge banana leaves . . .
    Mahout:* *'It's his lunch'*

       *ELEPHANT KEEPER AND DRIVER

(Bangalore)
   Tony restaurant . . .
ignored tropical orchids
   pull their little girl . . .

NEPAL
   The plateau of peace
and spirit, tilled with holiness,
   that Katmandu was . . .

Dawn in Kathmandu:
where all was glare before
is a glory, now

(Nepal Village)
On sunny doorsteps:
to each bare toddler — when caught —
a massage of oil and love

Treasured from Nepal:
the nudging farewell from that ox
with Buddha's eye

Zen alert! Red robes
amid old scrolls — encoding
a Way beyond words!

This sunrise flight
along the Himalayas
tears every eye

❖   ❖   ❖

EGYPT
Nile morning . . .
far bank, a misty 'Sesshu'*
here, pure 'Gauguin'

*JAPANESE ZEN PAINTER

(Aswan)
Deluxe hotel launch . . .
Tourists look away from a raft
full of staring eyes

For the braying mule
beaten into a gallop —
sympathy, Nile-wide

Nile enchantments!
Thanks to a rattling deck light
  I remain aware

Ragged Nile farmer:
still faintly gracing his cart
  youth's weathered design

Netting nothing,
the fisherman takes a stick
  and smacks the Nile

Along the Nile shore
a live gamboling performance
of 'kidding around'

Hidden by Nile reeds
til given up by a heron:
industry's anus

Floating belly up
between tour boat traffic —
a monitor lizard

(Temple of Luxor)
Gods long gone, now
the home of spirit and strays . . .
Destiny's design ?

Pharaoh's true treasure:
the way his empty tomb
now unites the world . . .

Lifting every lens —
'Here, god Ra in erection
creates the cosmos'

From the one temple
screened against birds . . .
avian concerts!

Temple of Karnak . . .
skulking round the great columns:
skittering shadows

As Nile dusk deepens
egrets blizzard to the same
solitary isle . . .

While peace plies the Nile
and awe tours the tombs, fear
rides our guarded coach

(Cairo)
All from two donkeys
pausing to nuzzle muzzles:
a concert of horns!

First the 'Cairo flu,'
now eye-seeking flies here at
Tut's tomb! Just maybe . . .

Muezzin* dusk . . .
Swinging censers cloud
and incense the souk

*MUSLIM CALLER OF PRAYERS

The censered souk
echoes my 'coughing Zen'. . .
asthma in Islam

A desert mouse
dares the bazaar, to drink
from an uneven tile

60

MOROCCO
Dawn over the Atlas . . .
plowing together as one
camel, mule, and man

Ancient Casbah wall:
a backrest now, hiding
ghostly rubble

(during Ramadan)
Sunset cannon:
busy Marrakech Square
empties with hunger . . .

(Marrakech)
Christmas in Islam . . .
not just in tourist hotels,
decorated trees
(1997)

Like Blyth, that farmer,
the way birds probe and wing
around his plow. . .
*REFERS TO R. H. BLYTH, HAIKU SCHOLAR

(Sahara)
Oasis rest stop . . .
Cheering us from a poster,
Stan and Ollie!

62

TUNISIA
Sahara sandstorm:
as road, desert, and mile markers
disappear — the fear!

Uganda leftovers:
gorilla hands — so who's
next on the menu?

❖   ❖   ❖

AT HOME

(Santa Cruz Mountains)
Back in our mountain home,
filled with those *'Glad I left ya,*
so long city, blues'

Spring garden . . .
ever attending its 'Zen concert'
my blessed wife

(Pacific Coast)
Wedded with time
like music — dew imbued
with its flower's hue

On a pollen high,
dancing the tarantella
  upon every bloom

Addressed as 'Cosmic'
this chameleon leaps up, clings
and now rides me home

Once riding the wind,
now drawing a cloud
  of bees and sand fleas

(Golden Gate Park)
    Among bamboo shoots
one expands the ring
    of an old condom

Dry El Niño year:
pianissimo at best
    our old roses 'concert'

Paradise gardener:
'See how we train our roses
    to flower the sky'
        (FOR PATRICIA)

Better than Matisse —
my garden's annual dance
of 'naked ladies'*

*AMARYLLIS BELLADONNA

Boy and tree long gone —
but not those plump Nihon plums
with their amber gems!

(REMINISCENCE, SEATTLE 1938)

Riding out waves
of compassion and despair
to just live and create

(HAWAII 2004)

67

Of abandoned roads
with weeds, grassy rails, and birds
my 'way' of haiku

❖   ❖   ❖

ABOUT THE POET

JAMES W. HACKETT BEGAN WRITING HAIKU IN ENGLISH IN THE
1950S WHILE IMMERSED IN THE WRITINGS OF ZEN PHILOSOPHER
D. T. SUZUKI. AFTER EARNING AN HONORS DEGREE IN HISTORY AND
PHILOSOPHY, A LIFE-THREATENING INJURY PROVED TO BE AN
EPIPHANY: IT LED TO INTENSIVE MEDITATION, AND THE PERUSAL OF
R. H. BLYTH'S RENOWN WORKS ON ORIENTAL CULTURE AND THE ART
OF HAIKU POETRY.

HACKETT'S POEM 'A BITTER MORNING /SPARROWS SITTING
TOGETHER/ WITHOUT ANY NECKS' BROUGHT INTERNATIONAL
RECOGNITION IN 1964 BY WINNING JAL'S FIRST AMERICAN HAIKU
CONTEST. ENCOURAGED AND PERSONALLY MENTORED BY DR. BLYTH
AND HAIKU SCHOLAR HAROLD G. HENDERSON, HE CONTINUED
WRITING. TWO BOOKS OF HIS HAIKU WERE BROUGHT OUT BY
HOKUSEIDO PRESS, AND SEVERAL OTHERS BY JAPAN PUBLICATIONS
(TOKYO). THESE YEARS ALSO SAW THE BEGINNINGS OF 'A TRAVELER'S
HAIKU' VIA TREKS INTO THE NORTH AMERICAN WILDERNESS, AND TO
JAPAN WHERE HE EXPLORED THE ROOTS OF HAIKU, AND WAS THE
GUEST OF NOTED ZEN ROSHI. HIS HAIKU HAVE SINCE BECOME WELL
KNOWN IN JAPAN.

WRITING CAN BE A RECLUSIVE, SOLITARY LIFE, AND THE POET
REMAINED DEVOTED TO MEDITATION AND TO WRITING MANY ZEN-
INFLUENCED POEMS (YET TO BE PUBLISHED). HACKETT WAS ALSO
ACTIVE IN THE WORLD HAIKU COMMUNITY, ADJUDICATING VARIOUS
HAIKU COMPETITIONS, SPEAKING AT HAIKU CONFERENCES IN THE USA
AND ABROAD, CONNECTING WITH GIFTED HAIKU POETS AROUND THE
GLOBE, AND WORKING TO FURTHER UNDERSTANDING OF HIS
SPIRITUAL 'WAY' OF HAIKU ('THAT ART THOU'). CURRENTLY HE IS
HONORARY PRESIDENT OF THE WORLD HAIKU CLUB (SEE WEB SITE).
SINCE 1990 THE BRITISH HAIKU SOCIETY HAS OFFERED 'THE ANNUAL
JAMES W. HACKETT INTERNATIONAL HAIKU AWARD,' ADJUDICATED BY
THE POET.

AFTER LIVING IN THE SANTA CRUZ MOUNTAINS OF CENTRAL
CALIFORNIA, HACKETT NOW SHARES A QUIET, CREATIVE LIFE IN HAWAII
WITH HIS WIFE PAT, AND A ROWDY, LOVABLE COLLECTION OF GOOD-
NATURED DOGS.

A TRAVELER'S HAIKU
旅人の俳句

2004年10月20日　初版発行

著　者　James W. Hackett

発行者　㈱ 北 星 堂 書 店
代表者　山 本 雅 三

〒 113–0021 東京都文京区本駒込 3–32–4
Tel (03) 3827–0511 Fax (03) 3827–0567

THE HOKUSEIDO PRESS
32–4, Honkomagome 3-chome, Bunkyo-ku, Tokyo 113–0021 Japan
URL: http://www.hokuseido.com   MAIL: info@hokuseido.com

◆ 落丁・乱丁本はお取り替えいたします。